CONTENTS

KT-440-353

WHAT'S THE PROBLEM?

We all know what an emergency is. We have seen pictures on TV or in the newspapers of buildings devastated by earthquakes, or people left homeless by war or floods. Maybe you have experienced a major emergency yourself – been present at a car crash or **evacuated** from a shopping centre during a bomb scare. But there are other kinds of emergencies too, personal emergencies, such as when an elderly person is too ill to do their own shopping or get to the doctor. All emergencies, however big or small, leave the people involved in them scared and **vulnerable** and in need of help.

In the devastating earthquake in Turkey in 1999, hundreds of people were injured or killed and many Turkish families were left homeless.

Disaster struck in October 1999 when two trains packed with people colllided and burst into flames near London's Paddington Station.

The recent increase in *natural disasters* is partly due to changes in the world's climate.

BRITISH RED CROSS

LOUISE SPILSBURY

www.heinemann.co.uk
Visit our website to find out more information about **Heinemann Library** books.

To order:
☎ Phone 44 (0) 1865 888066
▤ Send a fax to 44 (0) 1865 314091
💻 Visit the Heinemann Bookshop at www.heinemann.co.uk to browse our catalogue and order online.

First published in Great Britain by Heinemann Library, Halley Court, Jordan Hill, Oxford OX2 8EJ, a division of Reed Educational and Professional Publishing Ltd.
Heinemann is a registered trademark of Reed Educational & Professional Publishing Limited.

OXFORD MELBOURNE AUCKLAND JOHANNESBURG BLANTYRE
GABORONE IBADAN PORTSMOUTH NH (USA) CHICAGO

Designed by Ken Vail Graphic Design, Cambridge
Originated by Universal Colour Scanning
Printed by Wing King Tong in Hong Kong

Heinemann Library paid a contribution to British Red Cross for their help in the creation of this book.

ISBN 0 431 02738 2 (hardback)
05 04 03 02 01
10 9 8 7 6 5 4 3 2

ISBN 0 431 02744 7 (paperback)
05 04 03 02 01
10 9 8 7 6 5 4 3 2 1

British Library Cataloguing in Publication Data

Spilsbury, Louise
British Red Cross. – (Taking Action!)
1.British Red Cross – Juvenile literature
I.Title
361.7'634'0941

Acknowledgements
The Publishers would like to thank the following for permission to reproduce photographs:
All photographs © British Red Cross, with the exception of p 21 lower AusAid/David Hough; p22 Belfast Newspapers Ltd; pp25 left, 29 upper ICRC; p20 ICRC Agro program; p8 lower ICRC/Paul Grabhorn; p8 upper ICRC/Till Mayer; p9 lower ICRC/Heine Pederson; p4 lower Reuters/Popperfoto/Hugh Pinney.

Cover illustration by Scott Rhodes.

Cover photograph by British Red Cross/Howard Davies.

Our thanks to staff at British Red Cross for their help in the preparation of this book.

Every effort has been made to contact copyright holders of any material reproduced in this book. Any omissions will be rectified in subsequent printings if notice is given to the Publisher.

Words appearing in the text in bold, **like this**, are explained in the Glossary.

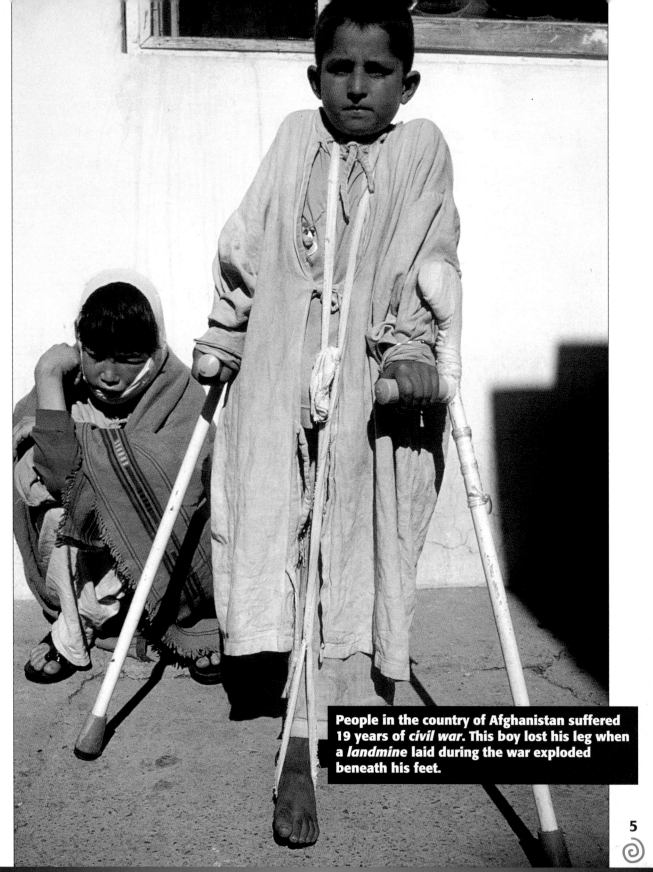

People in the country of Afghanistan suffered 19 years of *civil war*. This boy lost his leg when a *landmine* laid during the war exploded beneath his feet.

In Afghanistan in 1997 the Red Cross fitted over 3000 *artificial limbs* within nine months.

WHAT IS THE BRITISH RED CROSS?

In 1859 a Swiss businessman called Henry Dunant was in Italy at the time of the **Battle of Solferino.** The suffering of the injured and dying soldiers there was horrific. Thousands died because there was no one to help them. Dunant encouraged local people to work with him to help casualties from both sides. On his return home he came up with the idea of setting up groups of **volunteers** all over the world who would be trained in peace time to help the injured in times of war.

As a teenager Henry Dunant spent many hours with his family helping the sick, elderly and poorer people of Geneva, the city in which he was born. As an older man he had an even greater effect on people's lives.

At the terrible Battle of Solferino many of the 40,000 casualties died because there was no one there to tend to their injuries.

Henry Dunant was given the very first *Nobel Peace Prize.*

ORGANIZED AID

In response to these ideas a committee, which later became the International Committee of the Red Cross (ICRC), was set up in Geneva, Switzerland. In 1863 the Red Cross Societies began their work in countries around the world. The British Red Cross was founded on 4 August 1870.

Henry Dunant also suggested that countries should take part in an international agreement to protect victims of war. This became known as the **Geneva Convention**. Countries which sign later versions of this agreement make a promise to obey certain rules, such as not harming **civilians**, not mistreating prisoners of war and not attacking medical services which carry the red cross or red crescent emblem.

ANYTIME, ANYWHERE

From its small beginnings, Henry Dunant's committee has grown into the largest independent **humanitarian** organization in the world. Volunteers still support the military in times of war. But today Red Cross workers are also there to help people who face other emergencies and people who need help in their everyday lives – in their own homes, in local communities or anywhere in the world.

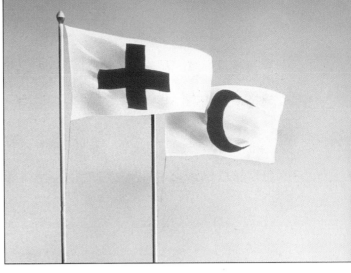

Some countries prefer to use the sign of the red crescent instead of the red cross. Both groups have the same aims and their volunteers work in the same way. Together they are known as the International Red Cross and Red Crescent Movement.

The Red Cross helps people in need in times of peace and in times of war, whoever they are, wherever in the world they are, and however different or difficult their needs might be.

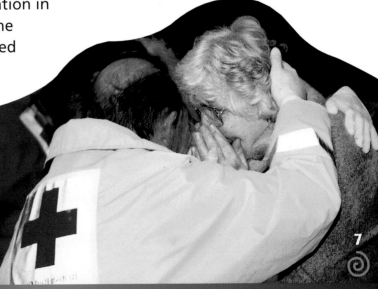

There are now over 170 Red Cross and Red Crescent Societies worldwide.

HOW DOES THE BRITISH RED CROSS HELP?

Would you know how to respond in an emergency? Would you have any idea what to do or how to help people? British Red Cross **volunteers** and workers do. They are trained to be ready to take action in emergencies of all kinds. This is called 'emergency response' and it is the driving force behind everything the British Red Cross does.

CARING IN A CRISIS

The British Red Cross helps in different ways depending on the kind of emergency. In the UK it provides services to help people with personal crises in their daily lives, such as driving patients to hospital for treatment. It also helps **local authorities** and the national emergency services, such as police, ambulance and fire services, when there is a major incident or disaster in the UK, for example a train crash or a flood. In times of a national emergency, such as a war, the British Red Cross assists the health services and armed forces.

In times of crisis the Red Cross enables trained people such as doctors, nurses or engineers to help those in need.

Sometimes the help that is needed in an emergency is equipment like tents, blankets, food and medical supplies. Here Red Cross workers are giving out emergency *food parcels* to families in war-torn Chechnya, Russia.

The British Red Cross has 68 branches working throughout the UK.

As part of the International Red Cross and Red Crescent Movement, the British Red Cross helps people all over the world in times of war, **natural disasters** or other crises. It also joins in a worldwide battle against disease, **poverty** and hunger – emergencies which are facing the world's most **vulnerable** people all over the world, all the time.

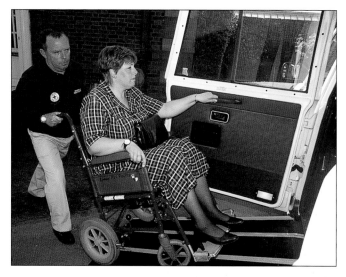

▲ Some crises are on a more personal level. For example, Red Cross volunteers drive people who would not otherwise be able to get about to the shops or to a doctor.

▶ In times of war or natural disasters people often have to leave their homes to find safety elsewhere. People may become separated from their families. The Red Cross provides an International Tracing and Message Service which helps people find and contact their loved ones again.

Red Cross and Red Crescent Societies work in their own countries and help each other.

MEET BOB STOREY
OVERSEAS DELEGATE

I've been working with the British Red Cross for ten years. At present I work in Turkmenistan, in the former Soviet Union, with the Red Crescent Society there.

This is a country with many **vulnerable** people and I'm here to help the Red Crescent develop various projects to help them.

I work with young people to organize youth clubs so they have somewhere to go to have fun and learn new skills. I also visit old and lonely people for a chat and to take them food. I like my job because as well as being able to help others and travel and find out about other countries, I learn so much from the different people I meet.

This is me meeting with members of the youth project I'm working on.

8am My first job of the day is to check my e-mail messages from the Red Cross offices in London and Geneva. It's important that the **charity** is kept informed of the work we're doing here.

9am I meet with the Head of the youth project I'm working on. We discuss plans for Summer Camp. The Summer Camp is for Youth Club members. They live together for ten days in tents and learn how to help the Red Cross in working on things like **first aid**, medical problems and distributing aid.

11am I go with the Red Cross Search and Rescue team to practise rescuing people from a collapsed building. Turkmenistan is prone to earthquakes and this training is part of the earthquake preparedness work the Red Cross is doing with the fire services.

The British Red Cross has 92 British delegates working in countries around the world.

> We travel through the desert landscape of Turkmenistan in this white jeep. It has both the red cross and red crescent emblems on it.

1pm I have lunch with the Chairperson of the local Red Crescent organization. We discuss the shortage of money for our 'Hot Food for Elderly People' project and talk about how to raise funds for this important work.

3pm I travel to the Red Crescent branch office in nearby Dhashouz to see the Youth Club at work. Today they are working on first aid training and rubbish clearance. This is important to stop the spread of disease by rats or dirty water.

> Lots of young people in Turkmenistan work with the Red Crescent Youth Groups. They help sick and elderly people as well as visiting orphanages to help other young people. These youth members are entertaining war veterans.

Overseas delegates bring food, water, shelter and medical help to those in need, and work on disaster prevention.

MEET MIKE WATSON

FIRST AID VOLUNTEER

As a **volunteer** I help the British Red Cross in my spare time. Every year I provide **first aid** at lots of different events. I cover races and competitions such as motor racing, horse jumping and football, and also events such as local galas. Sometimes I act as a first aider, ready to give treatment to whoever needs it. Other times I work on ambulance duty, assessing how bad injuries are and taking patients to hospital if necessary. I also train young people and adults in first aid. All of the jobs I do for the Red Cross are worthwhile and give me a great deal of satisfaction.

7am Today I'm on ambulance duty. The day starts early with a hearty breakfast. Then we prepare a nourishing packed lunch — first aiding is hungry work!

8am My two colleagues and I arrive at headquarters where we check the ambulance equipment before setting off for the local gala we will be covering.

10am We get an early call to the football field. A young 'Michael Owen' leapt for a cross-ball and collided with a team-mate. We check him over and give him some first aid at the scene, but decide to send him off to hospital.

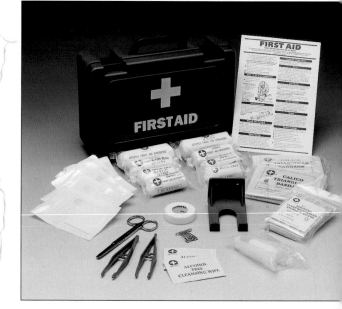

▶ **Before an event, I always check that the first aid pack has everything we might need.**

The British Red Cross trains more than 150,000

11am Most of the morning we are busy with minor injuries — a cut from a cola tin, a fall from a slide, a grazed knee, a bouncy castle bump, several wasp stings — and all before lunch!

2.30pm Things are a bit quieter after lunch so we take it in turns to walk around the field carrying our first aid pack. As we watch out for incidents we join in some of the games and the fund-raising.

6pm After taking an elderly lady with a suspected broken wrist to hospital, we drive back to headquarters in the ambulance. Then I head for home to enjoy a well-earned bath and a chance to wind down.

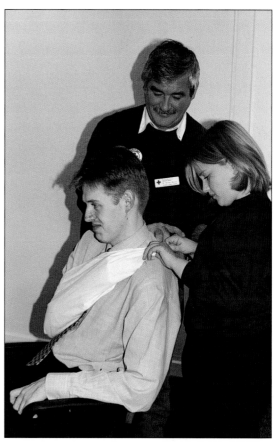

➤ **As well as my first aid duties I also train young people and adults in first aid. Here a young student of mine gets to grips with putting on an arm bandage.**

➤ **You get to meet all sorts of people when you are a volunteer! At one event I even met Mr Blobby – he was there to support the British Red Cross at a local event.**

Red Cross first aid training enables volunteers to

MEET CALLY SEYMOUR-SIMPSON

RED CROSS YOUTH MEMBER

Have you ever seen someone hurt themselves and wanted to help them, but didn't know how? Well, why not join a British Red Cross youth group? I did! I've been involved with various Red Cross activities for years and I really enjoy it. I've made lots of friends in my youth group, which mostly has people aged between 8 and 14. I've learnt **first aid**, infant and childcare, fire prevention, and casualty simulation, which was my favourite.

9am I'm up early for a Saturday because today our group is taking part in the Stevenage Carnival. We've got a float ready to compete in the Schools and Youth Groups category. We're going to make each other up using our casualty simulation skills.

10.30am I get out the make-up and the dough, ready for people to do their wounds. Then when everyone has arrived we're all busy — putting wounds on or trying not to fidget while being made up.

▼ **These are the wounded casualties we made up for the carnival. I did the nose job – it looks quite realistic, doesn't it?**

14

11.45am It's cold and we're hungry, even after eating our snacks, so we're really pleased when the judges come around and seem to be very impressed by our float.

12.30pm It's time for the float to drive around town in the carnival procession. Some of the members are up on the float while the first aiders walk alongside. They carry buckets to collect money for the Red Cross.

2pm We have to stop half-way around because someone up ahead has fallen off a float. It's times like this when I'm reminded how important British Red Cross first aiders are! We're wet and cold by now, but everyone seems to be having fun.

4.30pm After the procession we have a snack and then go to listen to the competition results. When the judge says 'In third place is... the British Red Cross' we're all very excited. It's been a brilliant day!

Adult Red Cross *volunteers* run camps for the youth members. They're great fun. Except for the washing up!

Youth members get the chance to be trained in

MEET JONATHON DAVIES

SERVICE USER

My name is Jonathon and I'm 29 years old. I've been having treatment for cancer since January 2000. I need to have treatment every day and the hospital I attend is about an hour and a half's drive away. I can't drive myself because the treatment is quite strong and leaves me feeling very tired and weak. So a British Red Cross **volunteer** driver drives me there, waits for me while the treatment is being done, and drives me back again. I'm really grateful to the British Red Cross for the help they've given me at this difficult time.

8.30am The British Red Cross driver picks me up from home bright and early. There are a number of different volunteer drivers. Today it's Gareth, who's taken me for treatment before. He drives for the **charity** every day.

▲ **Some British Red Cross drivers, like Gareth, drive their own cars. But the charity also has its own special vehicles, some of which are adapted for loading wheelchairs on board.**

10am We arrive at the hospital in plenty of time for my appointment. The volunteer drivers are always careful to get me here on time. British Red Cross cars have special parking places right next to the department I'm visiting, so I haven't got far to walk.

Each year the British Red Cross helps more than 350,000 people in the UK.

The British Red Cross is able to drive right to the entrance at most of the hospitals it works with. This saves time and means the patients don't have so far to walk.

10.30am After booking in at reception, Gareth and I go for a coffee while we wait for my name to be called for my appointment. The British Red Cross also runs the coffee shop at the hospital, so people waiting for treatment have somewhere relaxing to wait and have a coffee or a snack if they've had to travel a long way. Many of the British Red Cross volunteers here have special training in talking to people so they can discuss patients' treatment and their worries.

10.45am My treatment only takes 15 minutes, but afterwards I feel very tired. I'm glad to see Gareth waiting to walk with me back to the car and take me home again.

12.30pm We get home by lunchtime after a long journey. The journey is made easier because Gareth has been happy to talk to me about the treatment and how I'm feeling about it all. Even so, I'm glad to get home again and recover before the next day's treatment.

The coffee shop is busy today, but there are plenty of British Red Cross volunteers, trained in talking to patients and helping them to relax. Having someone to talk to is very important to many people suffering personal crises.

Red Cross volunteer drivers travel over 400,000 kilometres every year.

WORK IN THE COMMUNITY

Imagine it's 3 o'clock in the morning and your family has just lost everything they own in a house fire. You and your family are all safe, but you are cold and miserable and your nearest relatives live 500 kilometres away. In communities all over the UK, British Red Cross **volunteers** help people facing emergencies like this. They comfort them, find them clothing, blankets, food and drink, places to stay, or get them to other family members who can help.

CARING FOR PEOPLE

It is not only in times of fire or flood that the British Red Cross helps people like you. The **charity** provides many different services in local communities all over the UK. It responds to people's needs – and those needs change from one day to the next.

Volunteers help people with journeys they need to make, provide **first aid**, organize and deliver loans of medical equipment, such as wheelchairs, and give care at home when it's needed. Volunteers also work in British Red Cross shops, which are a vital source of income for the charity.

When you next go to a football match, fair or concert, look out for a Red Cross first aid post or ambulance. Red Cross volunteers trained in first aid are on standby to help at many such events, treating and comforting upset, unwell or injured people.

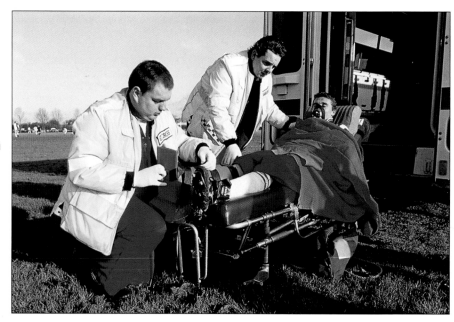

The British Red Cross makes over 250,000 loans of medical equipment each year.

VOLUNTEERS

Volunteers are at the centre of everything the charity does. Volunteers give up a great deal of their spare time and are usually ready to act at any time of the night or day, whenever and wherever they are needed. They have regular training sessions so that they know what to do in different situations. There are also paid staff who work for the British Red Cross but their job is mainly to support, organize or co-ordinate the work of the volunteers.

When someone is injured or sick they may need medical equipment, such as a wheelchair, back rest or walking stick. As they may not be able to get these from a hospital, the British Red Cross lends people what they need.

British Red Cross volunteers visit people at home. They may help with the shopping or look after someone while their usual carer has a holiday.

Each year more than 80,000 people volunteer for the British Red Cross.

WORK IN OTHER COUNTRIES

When a major disaster occurs in another country, many people read and hear about it and usually lots of help is provided. But what happens when the disaster is over and the floods have disappeared or the fighting has stopped? Families have been separated, children may have lost their parents, people are homeless, and there is a lack of food, medicine and water. People go on suffering. That is why the Red Cross goes on working all over the world all of the time.

CONTINUED SUPPORT

After the immediate crisis is over, the British Red Cross works with other National Red Cross and Red Crescent Societies to help local communities get back on their feet. They go on giving out **food parcels**, medical supplies, blankets, clothing and shoes, as well as finding places to stay for people forced out of their homes. They may even send out medical supplies for vets to treat farm animals to ensure food is produced in the future.

BEING PREPARED

Little can be done to prevent **natural disasters**. But people can be trained to be better prepared for when they happen. Red Cross and Red Crescent teams help communities organize early warning systems for people in areas of danger, build safe shelters, provide essential supplies and train people in **first aid** skills.

In times of war or natural disaster, livesto and crops are often ruined, leaving thousands of people without jobs or food. The Red Cross sends seeds and tools so familie can begin growing their own food again.

The British Red Cross is currently working in 34 countries across the world.

This means people will be ready to help themselves if and when they are faced with another emergency.

HEALTH AND MEDICAL SCHEMES

Providing people with clean water is one of the most urgent jobs the Red Cross does in times of emergency and in everyday situations. The **charity** also provides information about the diseases which can be passed on in dirty water. It works with countries to build better healthcare structures, for instance by helping local communities build new clinics or hospitals, or by providing medical supplies or extra doctors or nurses for existing hospitals.

First aid training is important. It helps people be prepared to help their families or others in their community in times of crisis and every day.

A supply of clean, safe water is something everyone needs to live, all the time.

£1 buys 20 litres of drinking water to help people in need.

WORKING WITH OTHERS

If you ever play football, netball or any other team game, you will know just how important co-operation is. If you work together as a team you have a much greater chance of success. People at the British Red Cross know this, too. They depend on support from **volunteers**, staff, and people who give **donations** of money. But they also need to work together with governments, other **voluntary agencies** and local organizations to provide the best help they can in any situation.

WORKING TOGETHER

On 15 August 1998 a bomb exploded in the town of Omagh, Northern Ireland, killing 29 people and injuring many more. British Red Cross volunteers worked with the **local authorities, social services** and police to find out where their help was needed most. Volunteers were asked to transport injured people to helicopters which took them on to hospital. They also helped the police deal with lists of missing people – sometimes going through lists of casualties to help people find out which hospitals their relatives had been taken to. Some volunteers helped **social workers** comfort people whose relatives had been killed or injured.

Although they could not avert the tragedy of the Omagh bombing, by working with others, British Red Cross volunteers brought comfort and help to many.

At Omagh, Red Cross staff and volunteers gave up their entire weeked to offer support to those in need.

HOME FROM HOSPITAL

Imagine returning home alone, after having an operation in hospital. You are weak and tired and may have no one to help you. To care for people in situations like this the British Red Cross provides a 'Home from Hospital' service. It works with local **health authorities** and other organizations to put volunteers in touch with people facing their first, difficult weeks at home. Volunteers may help them by doing the cooking or shopping, or by helping them in and out of bed if they have trouble moving about.

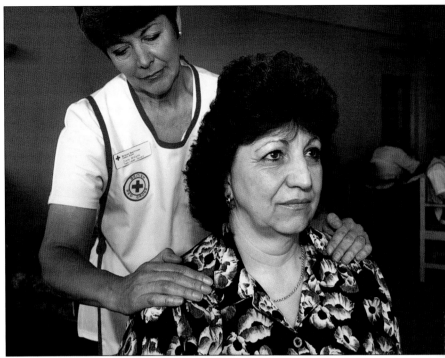

▲ Most of us find a massage relaxing, but it is especially helpful for people who are ill, and can even relieve their pain. British Red Cross volunteers help hospitals by visiting patients to give them simple hand, neck or shoulder massages.

► The Red Cross works with local authorities and other organizations to decide how best to help people. Some volunteers help people returning home from hospital, settling them back in and visiting them afterwards to see if they need anything.

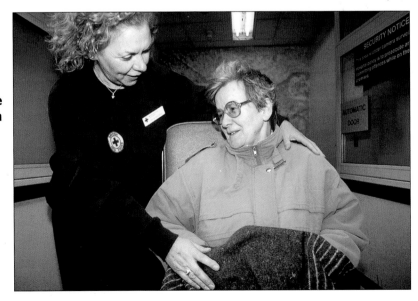

British Red Cross volunteers are ready to take action 24 hours a day, seven days a week.

WORK IN THE MEDIA

Turkish Earthquake

Hundreds of thousands of Turkish citizens have been made homeless by the worst earthquake this decade. The International Red Cross and Red Crescent Movement is helping to provide survivors with shelter, sanitation and medical assistance.

Make a donation HERE

or call: **0870 4443444**

or send a cheque, made payable to **'British Red Cross - Turkish Earthquake'**, to: **British Red Cross, Freepost, Turkish Earthquake Appeal, 9 Grosvenor Crescent, London SW1X 7BR**

British Red Cross

Caring for people in crisis

Registered Charity Number 220949

It is important for the British Red Cross to work closely with the **media**. By appearing in programmes we watch or newspapers we read, the **charity** can keep people aware of its work in the UK and abroad, and remind them that their **donations** of money are vital if it is to continue to do that work. The British Red Cross also needs coverage in the media to let the public know how it can help them, by telling people about the different services the charity provides in the UK.

LANDMINES

The British Red Cross uses the media to raise awareness of certain issues which are important around the world. Across the world millions of **landmines** have been laid during wars. When the fighting is over they are left in the ground. When people begin to use the land again, many are injured and some are killed by these hidden weapons.

When there is an emergency or disaster on a huge scale the British Red Cross produces adverts and posters like this to let people know what is happening and to ask them for donations.

On average one person is killed or injured by a landmine every 20 minutes.

As well as providing medical treatment and **artificial limbs**, the International Red Cross Movement has requested a worldwide ban on landmines. Over 40 countries have already agreed to stop using these weapons.

THE POWER OF HUMANITY

'The Power of Humanity' is the name of a five year **campaign** which the Red Cross Movement launched in May 1999. 'Humanity' means caring for your fellow human beings and the campaign aims to raise public awareness of the many ways in which the charity helps people all over the world. All 176 National Red Cross and Red Crescent Societies are taking part in this worldwide celebration. All kinds of activities, including poetry workshops, sporting events, dance shows and education programmes are going on all over the world.

PEOPLE ON WAR
CAMPAIGN ON INTERNATIONAL HUMANITARIAN LAW

INTERNATIONAL COMMITTEE OF THE RED CROSS

▲ As part of its landmines programme the **Red Cross is funding workshops which make artificial limbs so victims of explosions can walk again.**

▶ **A key part of the Power of Humanity campaign is the marking of the 50th anniversary of the signing of the 1949 *Geneva Conventions*. The International Committee of the Red Cross uses booklets like this one to remind people of the agreements made in 1949 and of their importance in the protection of victims of war.**

25

A child injured at the age of 10 will need about 25 new artificial limbs during their lifetime.

KOSOVO REFUGEE SUPPORT

The south-eastern corner of Europe is known as the Balkans. In the past many different peoples met here, in peace and in war.

This complex history is part of the reason why the states and countries of this region are so different, and why there has been so much trouble there in the past few years. In 1999 tensions between Albanian people in Kosovo and the Yugoslav government worsened. Kosovan people were forced or frightened out of their homes and their villages were destroyed.

EMERGENCY

Refugees from Kosovo fled to neighbouring countries Macedonia and Albania. When they arrived they were cold, hungry and exhausted. The first priority was to give them food, water and medical treatment. Planes sent by Red Cross and Red Crescent Societies also delivered tents, blankets, kitchen sets, baby packs and medicines. Cities of tents sprang up with many thousands of people needing comfort as well as the basic necessities of life.

REFUGEES IN THE UK

People cannot live in refugee camps indefinitely. The Red Cross and other **charities** worked together to find homes for the refugees in other countries. The British Red Cross supported some of those who came to the UK. **Volunteers** gave out essential items such as toiletries, food, cooking utensils, bedding and clothing and worked with **local authorities** to sort out financial help and find emergency homes. British Red Cross volunteers did all they could to help the refugees settle in the UK.

Around 800,000 refugees fled from Kosovo – that is about half the population of Northern Ireland.

This young Kosovan refugee is relaxing at a reception centre in Leicester. He is making friends and trying hard to settle into a new life in the UK.

The Red Cross tent was a sign of hope and comfort for the many refugees facing a cold Macedonian winter.

In some villages in Kosovo, nine out of ten houses have been destroyed.

VISION FOR THE FUTURE

In the future the Red Cross aims to be the leading voluntary provider of emergency help to those people in most need, anywhere in the world. The vision of the British Red Cross is for the red cross emblem to be the certain sign of hope for those in crisis everywhere. To achieve this aim the Red Cross depends on support from **volunteers** and staff, people who give **donations**, governments, **voluntary agencies** and fellow supporters across the world.

The *charity* guarantees that it will be ready to respond with whatever help it can when voluntary agencies or services like the police, fire or ambulance need its support.

One of the charity's most important jobs for the future is to identify the needs of *vulnerable* people and communities which are not being dealt with at present, and find ways of helping them.

► The British Red Cross will continue to show its commitment to supporting the International Red Cross and Red Crescent Movement all over the world.

▼ Supporters will continue to play a vital role in the charity's work and it will go on using the money they raise as efficiently as it can. These enthusiastic supporters are lowering themselves down the wall of a dam to raise funds!

FIND OUT MORE

If you would like to know more about the work of the British Red Cross contact:

The Information Service
The British Red Cross
9 Grosvenor Crescent
London SW1X 7EJ
telephone: 020 7201 5027
fax: 020 7245 6315

You can also find the British Red Cross on the internet. Look for us on:
www.redcross.org.uk
where you can find lots of information and material about the different kinds of work we do in the UK and in countries all over the world.

Shopping! If you are 13 years old or over you may be able to help out in a British Red Cross shop. There are hundreds around the country where second-hand goods are sold. Why don't you call in at your local shop and see what help they need? **Volunteers** sort clothes, serve customers and decorate the shop windows.

Fund-raising! We need lots of money to run the world's largest **humanitarian** organization. There are many ways you can help us raise funds. You could send a personal **donation** to the address above. Or you could get involved in a fund-raising event – from jumble sales to fashion shows, concerts to sponsored swims, there is no end to the list of events that you can get involved in to make money for the Red Cross.

Red Cross Week One week of every year is known as Red Cross Week. It is always the week with 8 May in it because this was Henry Dunant's birthday. During this week volunteers help to collect money by knocking on people's doors and holding tins in the streets. Everyone who makes a donation is offered a Red Cross pin to wear to show their support. Perhaps you could do a collection, with the help of an adult.

> You can take action too! Why not get in touch with your local British Red Cross branch to find out how you can help?

GLOSSARY

artificial limbs plastic or metal body parts which replace limbs lost by accident or injury

Battle of Solferino Napoleon III's victory over the Austrians in 1859 at a village near Verona, Italy

campaign/campaigning activities to bring about change

charity non-profit-making organization set up to help people in need

civilians people who are not fighting in a war

civil war war between groups of people living in the same country

donations gifts of money

evacuated when people are removed from a dangerous place to somewhere they will be safe

first aid help given to an injured person until full medical treatment is available

food parcels packs of food sent to people to sustain them in times of emergency

Geneva Conventions international rules for the protection of victims of war, first agreed in 1864, updated several times including in 1949, then extended in 1977

health authorities groups responsible for providing public healthcare services in different areas

humanitarian working to help other people

landmines bombs that explode when they come into contact with a person

local authorities local government groups responsible for organizing public services in different areas

media newspapers, magazines, radio, television, satellite and other forms of communication

natural disasters disasters caused by nature, such as floods, earthquakes, volcanoes, or hurricanes

Nobel Peace Prize prize awarded every year to someone who has done great work towards world peace

poverty not having enough money to buy the basic necessities of life, such as food, heating and clothes

refugees people who have had to leave their country and are afraid or unable to go back

social services services provided by the state for the community, such as education, health, and housing

social workers people trained to do work for the social services, helping provide people in communities with any help they need

voluntary agencies groups, such as charities, which are funded by donations and run mostly by volunteers

volunteers people who work without being paid

vulnerable people at risk because of their circumstances, such as poverty or old age

INDEX